The *Witch's Art*
of *Incantation*

Spoken Charms,
Spells, and Curses
in Folk Witchcraft

Roger J. Horne

Contents

Calling to the Green World

Love and Spurned Love

Coinage and Abundance

Curses and Maledictions

Spirit Flight and the Second Sight

Blessings and Benedictions

Introduction: Lingua Magica

In the mid-seventeenth century, Scottish witch Isobel Gowdie's words were believed to hold strange power. An utterance from her was thought by the authorities to spell sickness, doom, or dire misfortune to her victims. What might be a simple rhyme on the tongue of another was transformed, in her mouth, into a magical act, a machination of the witches' craft, darkly wondrous and full of potency. Whether Gowdie possessed any specific form of training in the witch's art of incantation is beside the point entirely. *Speech itself, in the witch's craft, is a magical act.* This, reader, is the fulcrum that binds the present volume, the exact aim and goal of this present work.

Today, we are both spoiled and plagued by representations of the witches' art of incantation all around us. Our fictive *wingardium leviosa*s and *bippity-boppity-boo*s have inured us to the very real craft of magical words left to us by our real ancestors. Even if one is so fortunate to come across a book with actual historic charms from the past, one must have a certain amount of knowledge and practice in order to make use of it. Yet, this wealth of lore is all around us, it seems. The barriers to achievement in spoken charm and incantation are not so much practical as ideological; most of us don't seem to know what to make of these archaic remnants or how to incorporate them into our practice. Modern witches, in the well-meaning work of creating new charms (that are, for certain, potent in their own right), are sometimes guilty of throwing the proverbial baby out with the bathwater, abandoning rather than preserving the very real and legitimate inheritance of incantations all around us.

Yet, for the folk witch, lore-derived practice is essential. Translating who our ancestors were and what they did into modern life is the heart and soul of the work we do. Folk witchcraft is, as a branch of the modern craft, decidedly personal, ancestral, and flexible, but remains firmly rooted in the witch-lore of the past. By following the truths and charms of our old lore, folk witches arrive at forms of modern witchcraft that make sense to our own individual locales, our familiar spirits, our spiritual ancestors, and our needs. Unlike Wicca, folk witchcraft has no inherent beliefs or structure because it is not a modern invention. Unlike some other forms of traditional witchcraft, folk witchcraft does not claim to hold the keys to an ancient esoteric brotherhood because it makes no pretense about the individual creativity and innovation of its adherents, whose practices have always varied by the contexts of time and location. Yet, this careful balance between the old and the new makes folk witchcraft one of the most open and welcoming branches of the craft. Those seeking a more thorough introduction to this branch of the craft may wish to consult my previous book, *Folk Witchcraft: A Guide to Lore, Land, and the Familiar Spirit for the Solitary Practitioner.* For the present volume, it is enough to understand that preserving historic charms is not merely an aesthetic decision, but an intentional piece of this form of witchcraft, and sharing these old treasures with other practitioners fills me with joy. It is my hope that witches of all walks of life will make use of the items in this volume, not in a dogmatic way, but in a way that quickens and inspires their individual magics.

In my personal collecting and experimentation with spoken charms, I admit to my own syncretist approach. For me, much like it was for my pagan and Christian ancestors, certain mythic figures seem to have a certain thematic union, even if their original names and worship come from different parts of the world. For this reason, I bring together charms associated with Hecate and Nicneven, Lucifer and Mithras, Aradia and Brigid. For the folk witch, finding the threads that spread across the Old Ones is an utterly natural form of folkloric analysis and a way to identify deeper wells of wisdom that run across our traditions the way springs across a mountain range draw from the same underground water source. There is nothing inauthentic here; our ancient ancestors themselves merged and collapsed their deities as they saw fit, finding joy and beauty in the ways the patterns of the Old Ones reproduce themselves across time and space.

Most of the magical language in this volume is translated either from another language or an archaic form of English, and I have taken varying degrees of license in order to arrive at workable charms that preserve the most potent aspects of the originals. Some of the charms here are originals, though in each case, they are based on folkloric tradition. Wherever possible, I provide the origins of the charm and a source that can be found either on the internet or via library collections. Witches exploring the incantatory arts are encouraged to read the original versions in order to revise, expand, or play with lexical approaches to their own personal charms. In the process, witches may discover additional historic charms not included in this work. This book offers merely a sample, and there are many other treasures waiting to be found.

I would like to note that the incantations and charms in this book are derived mainly from European and American sources because those are the locations of my spiritual ancestors, not because they are necessarily "better" or "more definitively witch-born" than any other sources. I hate few things as much as I hate the present false equivalence of genetics with magics that has become popular in gender essentialist and neo-nazi movements. In folk witchcraft, we are free to be ourselves, and the form of kinship we share celebrates cultural uniqueness rather than erasing it. Brujeria, stregheria, and fairy-doctoring can exist side by side as unique, equal, and connected branches of folk craft. In short, I believe that it is our responsibility as modern witches to both honor our past and embody a medicine against the long-standing curses we inherit from it.

The incantations included in this collection take many forms. Narrative charms involve recounts of folkloric tales and legendary events related to pagan and witch-lore. These are my own original work, but are firmly rooted in traditional lore and mythology. Other incantations are composed of modern reinterpretations of passages from the grimoires and magical texts of previous generations. I have done my best to include treasures from a variety of ancient and early modern cultures that speak to my interests and experimentation, but I make no claims to the completeness of this collection and openly admit to the absence of known magical traditions in Africa, Asia, the Middle East, and many other regions. In all honesty, it would be an injustice for a writer like myself, with no experience in these incantatory traditions, to attempt to represent them here. I do not think I could do it well. I do, however, strongly encourage other writers with roots in these traditions to do so. In folk craft, there is always room at the table, for the table can and should be built to the measurements needed by the people.

As you thumb your way through these pages, dear reader, imagine the voices preserved here. Think of all of these practitioners of old, their cacophony of speech, some perhaps having sat for hundreds of years in a yellowed, old tome, waiting for you. If you believe, like I do, that words hold their own peculiar form of magic, that they are living things coursing through our mouths and ears like blood, then the fact that you are holding this book now is no mere accident. Perhaps your own ancestors are there, reader, in the shadows of your room or behind a window-sill as you read this, listening for you to speak the old passwords. Accept this moment as a kind of initiation. Let these old charms wash over you and become a part of you. Learn what you can. Practice, revise, and alter them to suit your purposes. Feel yourself rooting into your vast and ancient family. Accept the precious inheritance of power sitting, even now, on the tip of your tongue.

Speak the old words, reader, and be heard.

Approaches to the Art of Incantation

The fact that all speech is a kind of magical act does not mean that merely speaking an incantation is enough to achieve a desired effect. There is an art to the spoken charm, and there are concrete strategies that the witch may employ to make this work more effective. At its heart, all incantation hinges on a trance-like awareness and deliberateness in the act of speech; everything from the tone, speed, volume, and airiness of the voice must be deliberate and purposeful. Likewise, if one is speaking a charm, we must ask: who is listening? Identifying (and sometimes constructing) the magical listener is the other half of the art of incantation, and one frequently overlooked. What is the setting for the spoken charm? What elements are at work in the witch's mind's eye as the utterance is made? All of these components play a vital role in this work.

To prepare for the performance of a spoken charm, the witch must make certain decisions in advance. What version of the witch's self is necessary to speak these words? Should the voice be dark and terrible? Kind and gentle? Stern? Aloof? Whose voice is this, and how can the witch best embody the traits needed to perform this successfully? This can affect everything from the clothing chosen for the incantation to the space used. In addition, the listener or target must be magically constructed. The witch should have a clear picture of this person in her mind's eye. Having a bit of hair or fingernails is even better. Having a poppet or handmade dolly resembling the target of the incantation is better still.

Witches who are new to the art of incantation might practice "seeing" their words travel through the air in the form of smoke or vapor, flowing out from between their teeth in search of the spell's target, circling them and surrounding them in the witch's mind's eye. Others may have success with visualizing their words taking form in the air around them, etching the incantation upon the deep. Last, but certainly not least, is the method known as spirit flight or journeying, which involves the witch leaving the physical body in order to visit the target of the spell. This can be useful for whispering the incantation directly into the ear of the victim, a potent way of planting words to take root.

In terms of the act of magical speech, much must be decided. The witch may wish to embody vocal alteration to take on some necessary quality. The voice may be dry and raspy like fall leaves on the wind or cold and emotionless as ice. Likewise, the delivery may be warm and soothing like a familiar friend. A whisper suggests intimacy and closeness, a force of influence that arrives slowly. A shout or yell is meant to frighten and arrest the target. A melodic or sing-song performance of the incantation is conducive to hypnotic effects. Speedy, cacophonous repetition gives the effect of one voice becoming many, surrounding the target, while a slow, intentional voice focuses the attention rather than overwhelming it. Words may also be pronounced forward or backwards, the latter producing a barbarized language that can render familiar words strange and disarming to the listener. None of these incantatory methods must absolutely be performed physically; the inner or deep voice may be used in any of the manners above without making a single sound in the physical world.

Incantation as Ritual

Many modern witches are surprised to find that medieval and early modern grimoires contain charms that are at times simple and straight-forward in their methods. What is not evident in these texts is the context in which previous generations would have approached barbarous words and magical language. Both Europe and the Americas was largely Christianized in the time of our cunning craft ancestors, and they would have felt a very real fear when calling on spirits identified as devils or even simply pronouncing words published in a forbidden magical text. That fear and anxiety would have been a very real source of energy empowering the mere act of incantation.

For these practitioners, and for us as modern folk witches, incantation is not merely a supplement to ritual, but can, when approached with great intention, be a ritual unto itself. By intentionally selecting the intonement and approach as outlined in the previous section, the incantation can be performed in any context, but more frequently, it is performed in a dedicated space. Darkness is most conducive to magical acts, and candlelight provides a focal point around the practitioner, reducing the plane of vision enough to grant intense focus only on the moment and task at hand. With practice, the candle itself can become a kind of simulacrum for the intended target, a focal point on which the witch can pour their attention and energy.

Still, many witches enjoy combining incantatory acts with other ritual acts constructed around a purpose, and luckily, there is no shortage of traditional and simple charms for the folk witch to employ alongside the chosen incantation. The following represent tried and true methods of the witch's contagious and sympathetic arts:

- The candle lit with intention, then snuffed out so that the smoke may travel out the window to seek its target.
- The candle stuck through with pins heated in its own flame.
- The poppet or dolly anointed with purpose as the target, then acted upon in various ways.
- The witch's ladder or cord tied with nine knots while focusing on the intention.
- The braid constructed from three cords while focusing on the goal of the working.

Some of the incantations provided in this volume are

intended to attain the attention of various entities. For land and nature spirits, it would be appropriate to perform the incantation in a suitable outdoor space. For conjurations of Old Ones (gods, ancestors, and lore-associated spirits), various spaces may be appropriate, so long as much respect is worked into the incantatory ritual. Other charms are aimed at triggering the "second sight" or initiating a session of "spirit flight." Witches unfamiliar with the practice of spirit flight may wish to see my previous guidance on this subject in *Folk Witchcraft*. In addition, many of the charms here given lend themselves to a particular season in the course of the year, and I encourage readers to pair them with meaningful days and times that are a part of their local folk traditions, incorporating them into native and personal practice.

However you make use of these incantations in your rituals, do so out of feeling and not dogma. Let your craft be rooted in the words of our ancestors, but make them your own. Listen to your intuition. Follow the guidance of your familiar spirits. Let the old craft be sustained and renewed.

Seeking the Old Ones

A Conjuration of the Queen of Elphame

White flower of the blackberry,
    fragrant flower of the apple,

sweet flower of the raspberry,
    summer in the cold stretch

of snow and barren trees,
    my pulse, my secret, my Queen.

Origin: Early Modern Period or before. Irish. Adapted and
rearranged with poetic license after *Reliques of Irish Poetry*.

An Adoration of the Moon

Hail to thee,
    bright moon of the seasons.

Hail to thee,
    bright moon of the waters.

Hail to thee,
    bright moon of the stars.

Hail to *thee,*
    bright moon of the path.

Origin: 1700s to 1800s or earlier. Scottish. Adapted and
rearranged with poetic license after *Carmina Gadelica.*

Another Adoration of the Moon

Hail to thee, thou round moon,
  jewel of guidance in the night.

Hail to thee, thou round moon,
  jewel of guidance on the billows.

Hail to thee, thou round moon,
  jewel of guidance on the ocean.

Hail to thee, thou round moon,
  jewel of guidance on the path.

Hail to thee, thou round moon,
  jewel of guidance of my heart.

May thy light be fair to me.
  May thy course be smooth to me,

thou fair lamp of grace,
    thou fair moon of the seasons.

Origin: 1700s to 1800s or earlier. Scottish. Adapted and rearranged with poetic license after *Carmina Gadelica*.

A Backwards Prayer to the Devil

Nema livee, morf su revilled tub
   noishaytpmet ootni ton suh deel sus

tshaiga sapsert taht yeth
   vigrawf eu za sesapsert rua

suh vigrawf derb iliad rua yed sith
   suh vig neveh ni si za thre ni nud

eeb liw eyth muck modngik eyth
   main eyth eeb dwohlah nevah

ni tra chioo, retharf rua.

Unknown antiquity. Grounded in Early Modern witch-lore of
various currents in the British Isles.

A Conjuration of the King of Elphame

There stand three trumpeters on the hill.
  Blow, blow, blow, winds, blow.

They blow their pipes so loud and shrill,
  and the wind shall blow thy spirit nigh.

I'll knit thee a finest linen shirt.
  Blow, blow, blow, winds, blow.

Without a stitch of needlework,
  and the wind shall blow thy spirit nigh.

I'll hang the shirt upon a thorn.
  Blow, blow, blow, winds, blow.

That by no son of man was sown,
  and the wind shall blow thy spirit nigh.

The thorn be watered from a well.
  Blow, blow, blow, winds, blow.

That never a drop or trickle filled,
    and the wind shall blow thy spirit nigh.

Origin: Sixteenth century or older. Scottish. Adapted and
rearranged with poetic license after *The English and Scottish
Popular Ballads*.

A Conjuration of the Light-maker

Origin of my origin,
    beginning of my beginning,

spirit of my spirit,
    water of my water,

fire of my fire,
    mixture of my mixture,

breathe into me
    that I may be born again

in thought,
    that I may wonder

at the sacred fire,
    O Great One of serpents,

of the lion and wolf.
    O flame-walker,

light-maker,
   fire-breather,

fire-feeler,
   light-breather,

luminous master,
   flaming body,

fire-sower,
   glorious light,

I am a star,
   wandering about you,

shining forth
   out of the deep.

Origin: First Century. Greco-Roman Egypt. Adapted and
rearranged with poetic license after *The Greek Magical Papyri.*

A Conjuration of the Luminous Lord of Serpents

Hail, serpent and lion of the fire.
    Hail, water and leaf-thick tree.

Hail, self-gendered one,
    invisible, fiery begetter of light.

Enter into this fire, and fill it.
    Let you who dwell within shine through.

Origin: First Century. Greco-Roman Egypt. Adapted and rearranged with poetic license after *The Greek Magical Papyri*.

To Implore a Favor
from the Queen of Hell

Hail, holy light, ruler of the depths of hell.
    Thrice-bound goddess, unleash your power.

O dog in maiden form, armed with swords,
    I adjure you by this potent hour of the night

in which the gates of hell are opened.
    I implore you by strange powers, healer,

swift-footed one, brave one, immortal,
    ghostly leader of nocturnal hosts, spinner

of fate, bright Queen, nethermost lady.
    By your symbols, your sandal, and your key,

cast the dark light from your eyes, she-wolf,
    fling open your thrice-locked doors

before your burning hearth, governess
    of the underworld, and take up thy powers

to aid me in this favor I ask of you now.

Origin: First Century. Greco-Roman Egypt. Adapted and
rearranged with poetic license after *The Greek Magical Papyri*.

A Conjuration of the Dark Queen of Wild Places

I reach for you, shining one of the night,
    triple voiced, triple-faced, triple-necked goddess

who holds and guards the untiring flame.
    Raise your dread voices in unity, O goddess,

your cry at which all things are shaken:
    every chasm, every mountain and valley,

every river, even the gates of the underworld.
    Blessed one, dart-shooter, huntress, beast-slayer,

come to me now from your feast among graves,
    with your triple heads of bull, horse, and wolf,

robed in black, lamp-bearer, mother of the people,
    dark Queen of gracious heart, hear my plea.

Origin: First Century. Greco-Roman Egypt. Adapted and
rearranged with poetic license after *The Greek Magical Papyri*.

A Conjuration of Our Lady of Beasts and Wilderness

I call upon you, lady of many forms and names,
    horned goddess who breathes sweet life

into every animal and plant, each living thing.
    Come, lady of the ox.

Come, lady of the vulture.
    Come, lady of the beetle.

Come, lady of the falcon.
    Come, lady of the dog.

Come, lady of the wolf.
    Come, lady of the serpent.

Come, lady of the horse.
    Come, lady of the goat.

Come, lady of the cat.
    Come, lady of the lion.

Come, lady of the mouse.
　　Come, lady of the deer.

Come, lady of the torch and key.
　　Hear me, O mighty one.

Origin: First Century. Greco-Roman Egypt. Adapted and
rearranged with poetic license after *The Greek Magical Papyri*.

A Conjuration of the Witch Queen

Commer, go ye before.
　　Commer, go ye.

If ye will not go before,
　　Commer, let me.

Ring-a-ring a widdershins,
　　a whirlin', skirlin' widdershins,

Commer, Carlin, Crone and Queen,
　　three times three.

Commer, go ye before.
　　Commer, go ye.

If ye will not go before,
　　Commer, let me.

Ring-a-ring a widdershins,
　　a whirlin', skirlin' widdershins,

Devil take the hind-most
   where er' she be.

Origin: Sixteenth Century. Scottish. Adapted and rearranged
with poetic license after *Newes from Scotland*.

A Conjuration of Mother Night

Mother night, from whom the first
    gods and spirits arose, silent queen

of ebony and rest, whose darkling
    coursers circle the earth, you whose train

of phantoms and shadows gather up
    the light and bury it: hear my call.

Twilight's blessed lady, hear me.

Origin: 3 BC - 1 AD. Greco-Roman. Adapted and rearranged
with poetic license after *The Hymns of Orpheus*.

A Conjuration of the Goat-God

Come, horned serpent, from your lonely glade
   and rejoice in melody. Come leaping,

come reeling, come furious and fearsome,
   ruler of all nature, all-fertile soul of the world,

and hear my plea. Come from your cave
   beneath the earth, rising like fire

to the summit of the azure sky,
   and with me, thy liberal bounties share.

Origin: 3 BC - 1 AD. Greco-Roman. Adapted and rearranged
with poetic license after *The Hymns of Orpheus*.

A Conjuration of the Maiden of Life and Death

Come, blessed queen, standing astride
    the black gates of hell.

Come, infernal queen, keeper of secret
    seeds within the earth.

Come, horned maiden of spring,
    whose face we see in budding fruits.

Come, dark mistress of autumn,
    whose will is the death of all things in time,

Hear my voice in thine ancient abodes.
    Illustrious lady, hear me.

Origin: 3 BC - 1 AD. Greco-Roman. Adapted and rearranged
with poetic license after *The Hymns of Orpheus.*

A Conjuration of the Goddess of the Moon

Huntress swift in course, torch-bearing goddess
    who presides over birth and creation,

bane of the enemy, maiden of loosed arrows
    who wanders by night through sky

and rejoices on wooded peaks,
    share the bounty of thy blessing, nurse

of human-kind. Illustrious one, fair
    and bright, hear my call.

Origin: 3 BC - 1 AD. Greco-Roman. Adapted and rearranged
with poetic license after *The Hymns of Orpheus.*

A Conjuration of the Mother of the Earth

Mother of seed and corn and fruit,
   of the oxen and the yoke, bounteous reaper

who wields the scythe and the flower,
   who waxes the increase of summer

and fills nature's stores of wealth,
   thresher of harvest, round-bellied queen,

attend me now and hear my call.

Origin: 3 BC - 1 AD. Greco-Roman. Adapted and rearranged with poetic license after *The Hymns of Orpheus*.

A Conjuration of the God of the Wild

O wild god of two-fold shape,
   O wild god thrice-begotten,

O wild god of the wooded hills,
   O wild god of the bull face,

O wild god of the vine,
   O wild god of the horns,

O wild god dark and fair.

Origin: 3 BC - 1 AD. Greco-Roman. Adapted and rearranged
with poetic license after *The Hymns of Orpheus*.

A Call to the Sun

You whose golden eye surveys all,
    lord of seasons within thy fiery cart,

foe of wickedness, hear me.
    You father of ages, flame immortal,

watchful rider of the skies, hear me.
    Lord of years, pulled by fiery steeds,

eye of the just, hear me. I conjure you
    and invoke thy mighty aid.

Origin: 3 BC - 1 AD. Greco-Roman. Adapted and rearranged
with poetic license after *The Hymns of Orpheus*.

A Conjuration of the Man in the Moon

Spirit of Cain, I conjure thee
    to know neither peace nor rest

from within thy lunar prison
    until thou grant my request.

May you run and beat your hands,
    yet find no bodily warmth until

you give some sign that this grace
    I ask of thee be granted.

Origin: 1800s or earlier. Italian. Adapted and rearranged with poetic license after *Aradia: Gospel of the Witches of Italy.*

A Conjuration of Aradia, First of Witches

By the hissing of a serpent,
    by the glimmer of a firefly,

by the croaking of a toad,
    I call to thee, daughter of the old one

who did become the king of hell
    and by his sister, the moon,

did sire forth the witches' line.
    Teacher, first of witches, I implore thee

to grant the request I ask of thee.

Origin: 1800s or earlier. Italian. Adapted and rearranged with poetic license after *Aradia: Gospel of the Witches of Italy.*

Another Conjuration of Aradia, First of Witches

At midnight, I walk into a field.
  Bless me with water, wine, and salt.

I go to seek after Aradia.
  Bless me with water, wine, and salt.

Daughter of the fallen angel,
  bless me with water, wine, and salt.

I implore this favor dire.
  Bless me with water, wine, and salt.

Origin: 1800s or earlier. Italian. Adapted and rearranged with poetic license after *Aradia: Gospel of the Witches of Italy.*

A Conjuration of the Darkling Wolf

In Ironwood did an Old One reside
and birth the brood of darkling wolves

to feed upon the flesh of the dead,
to redden the house of the gods with gore,

to bring the dark and rolling storms,
the greatest of these, strong in darkness,

destined to steal the sun from the sky.

Origin: 11th Century or earlier. Icelandic. Adapted and
rearranged with poetic license after *The Poetic Edda*.

A Conjuration of Old Nick

Devil, I conjure thee in the name
    of thy three golden hairs, which the good soldier

did pluck from thy head, and in the name
    of thy grandmother, who keeps thy house,

and in the name of the cauldrons in Hell's kitchen,
    boiling over their stoked fires in anticipation

of my oppressors, and in the name of thy three
    treasures: the corpse of an otter on the waves,

the rib-bone of a dead whale,
    and a horse's hoof to grace Hell's feasting table.

Original. Grounded in European folklore. See *The Devil with the Three Golden Hairs, The Devil's Grandmother,* and *The Devil's Sooty Brother* by the Brothers Grimm.

A Charm to Consecrate the Ground to the Devil

One, two, three, and four:
    the Devil knocks upon the door.

Welcome him from floor to roof.
    Drink to him in a horse's hoof.

Call the cat, the toad, the bran.
    Come to the feast, all ye who can.

One, two, three, and four:
    the Devil is here, so no more.

Origin: Early Modern. Welsh. Adapted and rearranged with poetic license after *Folklore and Folk Stories of Wales*.

Calling to the Green World

A Call to the Waters of Creation

And from that shining stream named Danu
　　that soaked the soil, and from

that great hazel tree, Bile, whose roots
　　fed that ancient salmon, did arise

all the forms and wonders of life. So do I call
　　upon that still pool to sustain me

and fill me with awe and wonder in each
　　form of the forest, hill, and glade.

Original. Grounded in early Celtic lore.

A Call to May and the Coming of Spring

Fair is May-time and noble summer.
    Fair, each great, goodly field.

Fair, the blackbird, singing.
    Fair, the long hair of the heather.

Fair, the smooth sea.
    Fair, the flowers covering the world.

Fair, the prickly hedge.
    Fair, the wood-harp's melody.

Fair, the waterfall greeting the warm pool.
    Fair, the speckled fish leaping.

Fair, the glory of the great hills.
    Fair, the echo in the valley.

Fair, the rushing of horses.

Origin: Ninth Century. Irish. Adapted and rearranged with
poetic license after *Four Old Irish Songs of Summer and Winter*.

A Call to Cold and Winter

Cold is the bed of the lake
    before the tumult of winter.

Keen is the wind, and bare is the hill.
    Cold is the bed of the fish.

White is the land where warriors rest.
    White is the hoarfrost, drifting snow.

The tree bows, and the snow
    covers the valley of frozen grasses.

Origin: Eleventh Century. Welsh. Adapted and rearranged with
poetic license after *Early Welsh Gnomic Poems*.

A Call to the Spirits of Trees

Oak, you are high above all others.
  Alder, lovely is your color.

Blackthorn, your sloe-bush is dark.
  Watercress, you are topped with green.

Saxifrage, you are the sweetest of herbs.
  Apple, you are shaken for your treasures.

Bramble, you are sated only by blood.
  Yew, you guard the graves of the dead.

Ivy, you are everywhere in the dark wood.
  Holly, you are a weapon in the hand.

Birch, lovely and smooth is your every branch.
  Aspen, you tremble and rustle.

Among your green will I make my home.

Origin: Twelfth Century. Irish. Adapted and rearranged with poetic license after *Buile Shuibhne*.

A Call to the Sea Winds

Here comes a great tempest on the ocean plain.
    The wind has arisen.

The spear of the wind flies across the sea.
    It passes over the broad, green sea.

The wind from the East rouses
    the mettle of the wave under the sun.

The wind from the North sets against
    the dark, stern wave, against the sky.

The wind from the West sets across
    the salt sea's rapid currents.

The wind from the South strikes
    against the rocks with its grey cloak.

Origin: Eleventh Century. Irish. Adapted and rearranged with
poetic license after *Otia Merseiana II*.

A Call to the Mists

Not a spot of land is to be seen,
    neither the birch-wood slope,

nor the shore, the mountains,
    the mist, nor the sea.

Like a cassock, the grey-black mist,
    a sheet without end,

the blanket of yonder, lowering rain,
    a black weft from afar,

hiding the world
    like a vapor from the ovens of Hell,

smoke of the ghost-fires of Hades,
    web of the spiders of the sky,

O father of the rain.

Origin: Fourteenth Century. Welsh. Adapted and rearranged
with poetic license after *Cywyddau Dafydd ap Gwilym a'i Gyfoeswyr.*

A Call to the Stars

Come, rushlights of the twelve signs,
    a shower to banish dire affliction.

Come, bright as sparks
    from the bonfires of seven saints.

Come, plums of the cheerless,
    frosted moon, hidden away.

Come, shield-rivets of the sky.
    Come, a swift wind cannot

dislodge you from your place.
    Come, pins in the headdress

of the great firmament.
    Come, clover-flowers

on the face of heaven.

Show me the valley and hill.

Origin: Fourteenth Century. Welsh. Adapted and rearranged
with poetic license after *Cywyddau Dafydd ap Gwilym a'i Gyfoeswyr.*

A Call to a Spring

Lovely is your pure-topped cress,
    the trout from your banks,

your wild swine in your thickets,
    the stags in your woods,

your dappled, red-breasted fawns,
    nuts on the crests of your trees,

the color of your young shoots,
    lovely brook of the hollow.

Origin: Twelfth Century. Irish. Adapted and rearranged with
poetic license after *Irische Texte*.

A Call to the Benevolent Plant Spirit

Hail be thou holy herb,
  plucked from the ground,

friend unto the people,
  in love and kinship bound.

Thou hast healed many a wound
  and soothed many a pain.

Awaken now to keep thy word
  in Our Lady's name.

Origin: Early Modern. Scottish. Adapted and rearranged with poetic license after *The Discoverie of Witchcraft*.

A Call to the Baneful Plant Spirit

Hail be thou potent herb
    plucked from the ground,

friend unto the poisoner,
    in wrath and vengeance bound.

Thou hast ruined many a lord
    and inflicted many a pain.

Awaken now to keep thy word
    in the Devil's name.

Origin: Early Modern. Scottish. Adapted and rearranged with poetic license after *The Discoverie of Witchcraft*.

Conjuration of the Snow Warrior

Hear my song and rise,
>   warrior of ice and snow.

Hear my song and rise,
>   horse and horseman of alder.

Origin: Unknown antiquity. Finnish. Adapted and rearranged
with poetic license after *Kalevala*.

A Call to Fire

Fire untamed, lustrous, and bright,
    power behind the sun, moon,

and every star. Aetherial fire,
    source of life, most splendid flower,

heat-bringer, light-bringer,
    hear me, radiant fire.

Origin: 3 BC - 1 AD. Greco-Roman. Adapted and rearranged
with poetic license after *The Hymns of Orpheus*.

A Call to the World Tree

I know an Ash tree between the worlds.
  Clean water nourishes its roots,

gives birth to the dew of the fields,
  ever growing green, kept by three maidens

strong in craft and wisdom.
  Laws they weave there, portions of fate

fixed to all the children of the earth.

Origin: 11th Century or earlier. Icelandic. Adapted and
rearranged with poetic license after *The Poetic Edda.*

Love and Spurned Love

A Charm to Incite Desire

Io torum cultin. Come to me, beloved.
Io torum cultorum. Come to me, beloved.

Io torum bultin. Come to me, beloved.
Io torum bultorum. Come to me, beloved.

Origin: 1700s. French. Adapted and rearranged with poetic license after *The Grimoirium Verum.*

Another Charm to Incite Desire

I conjure thee, O moon and stars,
  light held in my very own hand,

by the air within my lungs, and by the soil
  upon which I stand, and by all the names

of the spirits and principalities that bear
  upon you, and in the names of Mercurio,

Michiael, and Melchidael, to incite such great
  desire in [Name] that they can feel

no indifference towards me, only need,
  and when this work is finished, depart thou,

guardians of the moon and stars, in the names
  of Melchidael, Baresches, Zazel, Firiel,

and Malcha, and with my gratitude and love.

Origin: 1700s. French. Adapted and rearranged with poetic
license after *The Grimoirium Verum.*

A Charm for Love

My sweetheart waits
  atop the hill.

A rose of red
  and a rose of white.

The red rose drops
  its petals.

The white rose is
  my own true love.

Origin: Seventeenth Century. Welsh. Adapted and rearranged
with poetic license after *Penillion Telyn*.

A Charm for One Sought After

Once, the dark Queen lit three candles
　　on a high mountain beside the sea

to call the king unto three kingdoms
　　before the mist upon the bays,

the fruit trees, the brightly colored stones.
　　So, too, do I call the one I seek

in that lady's name.

Origin: Seventeenth Century. Irish. Adapted and rearranged
with poetic license after *The Poems of Egan O'Rahilly.*

A Charm to Pursue One Desired

My love was propped in the bower door,
  straight as a willow wand,

and then I called unto the heart
  with the hammer in my hand.

My love became a turtle dove
  to fly upon the air,

and I became another dove,
  flying pair and pair.

My love transformed into an eel,
  swimming in a lake,

and I became a speckled trout
  to kiss that eel awake.

My love changed then into a ship
  to sail over a flood,

and I became a nail therein
    embedded in its wood.

Origin: Sixteenth century or older. Scottish. Adapted and
rearranged with poetic license after *The English and Scottish
Popular Ballads*.

A Curse to Dissolve a Union

Woe and flame, woe and flame.
   I lay quarrel and strife between them.

Peace be unknown to their hearts.
   A monstrous body, a soul of flame,

the mountains pouring forth their tongues
   to scorch and burn these lovers' hearts.

Origin: First Century. Greco-Roman Egypt. Adapted and
rearranged with poetic license after *The Greek Magical Papyri*.

The Curse of the Nine Sea-Women

Nine women came to meet King Ruadh
in the land beneath the waves

to offer him their nine golden treasures
and bear his son.

The king broke his promise to them,
and all were dashed against the stones.

Thus does the traitor earn his treasure
at the fate of these nine.

Thus do I call nine hearts turned
from love to hatred against the enemy,

to carry out his cold reward.

Origin: Ninth Century. Irish. Adapted and rearranged with
poetic license after *Compert Con Culainn.*

A Chant to Undo Wrath and Sorrow

Hacedion
    hachedion.

Hacedion
    hachedion.

[Repeat]

Origin: 16th century. English. Adapted and rearranged with poetic license after Folgers Manuscript V.b.26.

A Charm to Soothe Wrath

I shall give you rest from wrath
    and soothe the pain of your rage.

I shall melt all anger and ill temper.
    Come, spirit of my enemy, in silence,

bearing silence, keeping silence,
    and taking silence back to your house

as surely as I am speaking to you now.

Origin: First Century. Greco-Roman Egypt. Adapted and
rearranged with poetic license after *The Greek Magical Papyri*.

A Charm to Turn the Wheel of Fate

And so Diana, by her witchcraft
    charmed her brother to lay with her.

And so Aradia, the first witch, was conceived.
    And when Lucifer found that his light

had been conquered by the darkness,
    he grew furious with rage at her trickery,

but she sang him a spell, a song of power,
    and he was silent; the song of the night,

against which he could say nothing.
    This was the first fascination:

a song hummed by the Moon,
    a spinning wheel, a buzzing of bees.

Diana spun the lives of all men,
    and Lucifer turned the wheel.

So do I grasp this wheel of fate
    and turn it in their names.

Origin: 1800s or earlier. Italian. Adapted and rearranged with poetic license after *Aradia: Gospel of the Witches of Italy*.

Coinage and Abundance

A Charm of the Three Spinners

Ye three spinners, hear me. Ye three spinners,
    I call out for your aid. Here comes the first

with her hefty foot to press the pedal. Lovely lady,
    hear me. Here comes the second

with her extended thumb to guide the thread.
    Lovely lady, hear me. And here comes the third

with her cleft lip to draw the yarn. Stand
    beside me, lovely dames of fate,

and I will not forget or deny thee thy fair due.

Original. Grounded in European folklore. See *The Three Spinners*
by the Brothers Grimm.

A Charm of Abundance

Here is my house in the wood.
    It is here, though none may know it.

Beside it, a bountiful tree of apples,
    a fresh stream splendid to drink,

swine, deer, and goats,
    fruits of rowan, black sloes,

a clutch of eggs, honey, bog-berries,
    strawberries, blackberries, acorns,

all in delicious abundance.

Origin: Tenth Century. Irish. Adapted and rearranged with
poetic license after *Hermit and King*.

A Charm of Prosperity

I have a house far in the North.
  Half is red-gold, and half is silver.

Its porch is bronze and copper.
  Its candlesticks made from gold

and shining, precious stones.
  A household without age,

a chess-game without end,
  a door closed to no one.

Origin: Thirteenth Century. Irish. Adapted and rearranged with poetic license after *Silva Gadelica*.

A Chant for Gain

Chaunta, Ferala,
　　Sadain, If, Guth,

Temterans, Tagam,
　　Seranna, Ferunt,

Eritherem, Elibanoth,
　　Nerohin.

Origin: 17th Century. French. Adapted and rearranged with poetic license after *The Grimoirium Verum.*

A Blessing of Abundance

We shall have flesh. It were enough.
We shall have hen. It were enough.

We shall have mead. It were enough.
We shall have wine. It were enough.

We shall have feast. It were enough.
We shall have sweetness. It were enough.

We shall have milk. It were enough.
We shall have honey. It were enough.

We shall have ambrosia. It were enough.
We shall have harp. It were enough.

We shall have lute. It were enough.
We shall have horn. It were enough.

We shall have lyre. It were enough.

Origin: 1700s to 1800s or earlier. Scottish. Adapted and
rearranged with poetic license after *Carmina Gadelica*.

A Charm for Increase in Riches

Saradon, I call you. I will call you Sarietur.
  Spirit Sadies, come to my aid.

Spirit Satani, come to my aid.
  Spirit Agir fons toribus, come to my aid.

Spirit Saradon, come to my aid.
  Spirit Saradon, whom I will call Sarietur,

Come to my aid. Speak to me the means
  to increase my wealth.

Origin: 1700s. French. Adapted and rearranged with poetic license after *The Grimoirium Verum.*

A Latinate Charm for Fruitful Business Endeavors

Odisti omnes, qui operantur iniquitatem:
  perdes omnes, qui loquuntur mendacium.

Virum sanguinum et dolosum
  abominabitur dominus.

Domine deduc me in iustitia tua:
  propter inimicos meos dirige

in conspectu tuo viam meam.
  Sepulchrum patens est guttur eorum,

linguis suis dolose agebant, iudica illos deus.
  Decidant a cogitationibus suis, secundum

multitudinem impietatum eorum expelle eos,
  quoniam irritaverunt te domine.

Quoniam tu benedices iusto. Domine,
   ut scuto bonae voluntatis tuae coronasti nos.

Origin: 5th century B.C.E. Pagan, Canaan. Adapted and rearranged with poetic license after the *Book of Psalms* (Vulgate) and the *Sixth and Seventh Books of Moses*.

A Latinate Charm for Influence and Popularity

Domine quis habitabit in tabernaculo tuo?
  Aut quis requiescet in monte sancto tuo?

Qui ingreditur sine macula, et operatur iustitiam.
  Qui loquitur veritatem in corde suo,

qui non egit dolum in lingua sua:
  Nec fecit proximo suo malum,

et opprobrium non accepit
  adversus proximos suos.

Qui pecuniam suam non dedit
  ad usuram, et munera super innocentem

non accepit: qui facit haec, non movebitur
   in aeternum.

Origin: 5th century B.C.E. Pagan, Canaan. Adapted and
rearranged with poetic license after the *Book of Psalms* (Vulgate)
and the *Sixth and Seventh Books of Moses*.

A Latinate Charm to Achieve Honor and Success

Indutus est dominus fortitudinem,
    et praecinxit se. Etenim firmavit orbem

terrae, qui non commovebitur.
    Parata sedes tua ex tunc: a saeculo tu es.

Elevaverunt flumina domine: elevaverunt flumina
    vocem suam. Elevaverunt flumina

fluctos suos, a vocibus aquarum multarum.
    Mirabiles slationes maris, mirabilis in altis
dominus.

Testimonia tua credibilia facta sunt nimis:
    domum tuam decet sanctitudo domine

in longitudinem dierum.

Origin: 5th century B.C.E. Pagan, Canaan. Adapted and rearranged with poetic license after the *Book of Psalms* (Vulgate) and the *Sixth and Seventh Books of Moses*.

A Latinate Charm for Favor in Legal Matters

Levavi oculos meos in montes,
unde veniet auxilium mihi.

Non det in commotionem pedem tuum:
neque dormitet qui custodit te.

Per diem sol non uret te:
neque luna per noctem.

Dominus custodit te ab omni malo:
custodiat animam tuam dominus.

Dominus custodiat introitum tuum,
et exitum tuum: ex hoc nunc,

et usque in saeculum.

Origin: 5th century B.C.E. Pagan, Canaan. Adapted and
rearranged with poetic license after the *Book of Psalms* (Vulgate)
and the *Sixth and Seventh Books of Moses*.

Curses and Maledictions

An Infernal Malediction

To the dark slough beyond the gates
    of hell do I deliver you.

To the maggots and beetles.
    To the jaws of the beasts: lions, dragons,

tigers, scorpions, and hawks.
    To the machinery of torment:

mallets, flails, swords, red spears,
    stench-fires, poison, and pits of sorrow

do I deliver my enemy.

Origin: Twelfth Century. Irish. Adapted and rearranged with
poetic license after *Lives of the Saints from the Book of Lismore*.

The Curse of the Tithe of Wrath

And I will go unto the mountain.
  And I will make the tithe of wrath.

And I will burn prickles and thorns.
  And I will set the cloud of smoke.

Like Cain who slew his brother
  will I make this dread offering.

Not in my name, but in the name
  of my enemy will I make it

that the wrath of the spirit
  be poured out upon him.

Origin: Seventeenth Century. Cornish. Adapted and rearranged
with poetic license after *Gwreans an Bys*.

A Charm to Reveal a Thief

Ye seven devils, I conjure you
    to reveal and set against the thief.

Anazarda Arogani, I conjure you.
    Labilafs, I conjure you.

Parandome, I conjure you.
    Azigola, I conjure you.

Maractatam, I conjure you.
    Siranday Eptalelon, I conjure you.

Lamboured, I conjure you.
    Reveal my enemy, and assist me.

Origin: 1700s. French. Adapted and rearranged with poetic
license after *The Grimoirium Verum*.

The Charm of the Witch's Nail

Nail, I conjure you in the name
    of the best and worst nail upon the ark,

bore from a hole the shipwright left
    that gave home to that old serpent,

whose body wedged between the boards
    sealed the wood and held the curse.

Origin: Sixteenth Century. Irish. Adapted and rearranged with poetic license after *Eriu*.

A Wasting Curse

And in that thunder did Old Polly Searce appear
    to curse the body of Vergil's love

that she might waste to bone and sinew
    lying in her bed for weeks, unable to move

even to lift her withering frame. So, too, do I curse
    the flesh of my enemy to utter waste.

Origin: Most likely 1800s. American. Adapted and rearranged
with poetic license after *The Silver Bullet*.

A Red Paternoster

Red Paternoster,
    Abel's dear brother.

One for the sickle
    and two for the reaper.

Three for the angel
    who suffers no master.

I conjure, I conjure
    O Red Paternoster.

Original. Grounded in Early Modern Scottish folklore.

A Charm for Power over the Enemy

Power of wind I have over thee.
  Power of wrath I have over thee.

Power of fire I have over thee.
  Power of thunder I have over thee.

Power of lightning I have over thee.
  Power of storms I have over thee.

Power of moon I have over thee.
  Power of sun I have over thee.

Power of stars I have over thee.
  Power of firmament I have over thee.

Origin: 1700s to 1800s or earlier. Scottish. Adapted and
rearranged with poetic license after *Carmina Gadelica*.

The Curse of the Singing Bone

By hollow reed and palest flute
    do I conjure the bones of the wronged

to speak and be heard. Speak, bones,
    against the murderous fiend, the traitor

brother, the wicked and blackened heart.
    Sing, flute of bone, in the every thought

of the enemy, a tone bent of breath and blood
    to beat against the walls of his skull.

Original. Grounded in European folklore. See *The Singing Bone* by the Brothers Grimm.

A Call to the Spirits of Ravens

Three ravens sat upon a tree,
   each as black as they could be.

One of them said to his mates,
   "Where shall we our breakfast take?

Down in yonder greenest field
   lies a fell knight under his shield."

Origin: Sixteenth century or older. English. Adapted and
rearranged with poetic license after *The English and Scottish
Popular Ballads.*

A Poisoner's Charm

And the Diana said to her daughter,
    'Thou shalt be the first of witches known,

and thou shalt teach the poor and oppressed
    such potent poisons and curses

to bind the great lords in their palaces,
    to ruin their crops and lay low their towers,

to rebuke priests and nobility in my name,
    the queen of witches all, and by my arts,

to sweep away these evil men.
    Ill the fate of those who do ye wrong.'

Origin: 1800s or earlier. Italian. Adapted and rearranged with
poetic license after *Aradia: Gospel of the Witches of Italy.*

A Charm by Playing Cards

I lay not forty cards on the table.
   I lay forty dread and mighty spirits

with power over the work of the body,
   the churning of blood, the labors of flesh,

power over the phantoms of the mind,
   the seeds of fear, love, and desire,

and power over the longings of the soul.
   Come ye now, forty cards,

and become ye forty devils.

Origin: 1800s or earlier. Italian. Adapted and rearranged with
poetic license after *Aradia: Gospel of the Witches of Italy.*

A Call to the Vengeful Dead

Here comes a ship on the northern sea
    carrying all the souls in Hell,

its queen at the helm, fair and dark,
    a scourge upon the branches of trees,

a throng of the dead upon the crags
    to cleave apart heaven itself,

to turn the red sun black as shadow,
    to sink the white-hot stars,

to raise fire from the belly of the earth.

Origin: 11th Century or earlier. Icelandic. Adapted and
rearranged with poetic license after *The Poetic Edda.*

A Hag-riding Curse

As the witch of Truro did force the bit
    into the mouth of Sylvatus

and did ride that captain across
    the crags and dunes of her own land,

pulling the reins to master him,
    denying him all sleep and rest,

so, too, do I master my enemy
    and torment his every moment of dreaming.

Origin: Most likely 1800s. American. Adapted and rearranged
with poetic license after *The Silver Bullet.*

A Latinate Charm against Thieves

Lex domini immaculata convertens animas:
 testimonium domini fidele,

sapientiam praestans parvulis.
 Timor domimi sanctus, permanens in

saeculum saeculi: iudicia domini vera,
 iustificata in sementipsa.

Delicta quis intelligit? Ab occultis meis
 munda me: et ab aliens parce servo tuo.

Si mei non fuerint dominati tunc immaculatus
 ero: et emundabor a delicto maximo.

Et erunt ut complaceant eloquia oris mei:
 et meditatio cordis mei in conspectu tuo semper.

Domine adiutor meus, et redemptor meus.

Origin: 5th century B.C.E. Pagan, Canaan. Adapted and rearranged with poetic license after the *Book of Psalms* (Vulgate) and the *Sixth and Seventh Books of Moses.*

A Latinate Charm to Silence Slander

Quoniam tamquam foenum velociter arescent:
    et quemadmodum olera herbarum cito decident.

Quoniam qui malignantur, exterminabuntur:
   sustinentes autem dominum, ipsi hereditabunt
terram.

Et adhuc pusillum et non erit peccator:
    et quaeres locum eius et non invenies.

Gladium evaginaverunt peccatores:
    intenderunt arcum suum.

Ut deiiciant pauperem et inopem:
    ut trucident rectos corde.

Gladius eorum intret in corda ipsorum:
    et arcus eorum confringatur.

Origin: 5th century B.C.E. Pagan, Canaan. Adapted and
rearranged with poetic license after the *Book of Psalms* (Vulgate)
and the *Sixth and Seventh Books of Moses*.

A Latinate Charm for Victory over the Enemy

Exaudi deus deprecationem meam:
   intende orationi meae.

A finibus terrae ad te clamavi: dum anxiaretur
   cor meum, in petra exastasti me. Deduxisti me,

quia factus es spes mea: turris fortitudinis
   a facie inimici.

Inhabito in tabernaculo tuo in saecula:
   protegar in velamento alarum tuarum.

Origin: 5th century B.C.E. Pagan, Canaan. Adapted and
rearranged with poetic license after the *Book of Psalms* (Vulgate)
and the *Sixth and Seventh Books of Moses.*

A Latinate Charm to Terrify Malignant Spirits

Exibit spiritus eius, et revertetur in terram suam:
    in illa die peribunt omnes cogitationes eorum.

Dominus illuminat caecos. Dominus erigit elisos.
    Dominus diligit iustos. Qui fecit caelum

et terram, mare, et omnia, quae in eis sunt.

Origin: 5th century B.C.E. Pagan, Canaan. Adapted and
rearranged with poetic license after the *Book of Psalms* (Vulgate)
and the *Sixth and Seventh Books of Moses*.

A Terrible Latinate Curse

Corrupti sunt, et abominabiles facti sunt in
    iniquitatibus: non est qui faciat bonum.

Omnes declinaverunt, simul inutiles facti sunt:
    non est qui faciat bonum, non est usque ad unum.

Quoniam deus dissipavit ossa eorum qui hominibus
    placent: confusi sunt, quoniam deus sprevit eos.

Quoniam alieni insurrexerunt adversum me, et fortes
    quaesierunt animam meam: et non proposuerunt

deum ante conspectum suum.
    Averte mala inimicis meis: et in veritate

tua disperde illos. Quoniam ex omni
    tribulatione eripuisti me: et super inimicos

meos despexit oculus meus.

Origin: 5th century B.C.E. Pagan, Canaan. Adapted and rearranged with poetic license after the *Book of Psalms* (Vulgate) and the *Sixth and Seventh Books of Moses*.

A Chant to Turn Back the Workings of the Enemy

Contere brachia iniqui rei
    et lingua maligna subvertetur.

Contere brachia iniqui rei
    et lingua maligna subvertetur.

[Repeat]

Origin: Early Modern. Scottish. Adapted and rearranged with poetic license after *The Discoverie of Witchcraft*.

A Charm of Unmaking

Abaxacatabax

Abaxacataba

Abaxacatab

Abaxacata

Abaxacat

Abaxaca

Abaxac

Abaxa

Abax

Aba

Ab

A

Origin: 19th Century. American. Adapted and rearranged with poetic license after *The Long Lost Friend*.

A Chant for Victory and Vengeance

Bachionodo
  balizlior.

Bachionodo
  balizlior.

[Repeat]

Origin: 16th century. English. Adapted and rearranged with
poetic license after Folgers Manuscript V.b.26.

A Chant to Identify a Thief

Bero barto bartoras
    quinquiel consuratur est.

Bero barto bartoras
    quinquiel consuratur est.

[Repeat]

Origin: 16th century. English. Adapted and rearranged with
poetic license after Folgers Manuscript V.b.26.

Spirit Flight and the Second Sight

A Charm for Admittance to Elphame

Twenty-eight warriors did Cailte see
    beneath the eldritch hill.

Twenty-eight lovely ladies there,
    six gentle youths in cloaks,

a maiden thrumming a harp.
    "Go and fetch the son of Cumhall,"

said one, "For Finn's house shall not
    be turned away from our court."

In Finn's name do I seek entrance,
    for friendship, honor, and grace,

to dwell in Elphame for a time.

Origin: Twelfth Century. Irish. Adapted and rearranged with poetic license after *Irische Texte.*

A Charm for Crossing Over

A traveller came to a river in a valley
    with many a fair, fine meadow.

A flock of white sheep on one side,
    and a flock of black sheep on the other.

When a white sheep bleated,
    a black one would cross over,

and when a black sheep bleated,
    a white one would cross over.

Black to white and white to black,
    changed in the crossing of the river.

Now do I come to call you over.

Origin: Twelfth Century. Welsh. Adapted and rearranged with
poetic license after *The White Book Mabinogion*.

A Charm for Scrying

Open my eyes. Open my eyes.
   Great serpent of the East,

dawn-riser, great craftsman,
   open to me this vessel of flame

upon the primeval waters.
   Speak to me through this mouth,

and let my cup reflect that
   which lies in the heavens.

Origin: First Century. Greco-Roman Egypt. Adapted and
rearranged with poetic license after *The Greek Magical Papyri*.

A Charm to Summon the Sight

The sign of sight I make on thee
    by Mary of the augury,

By Brigid of the corslet,
    and by Janet's foster,

those three great masters of cunning,
    by the imps of the storm,

by the spirits of the air,
    by the bones of the earth.

Origin: 1700s to 1800s or earlier. Scottish. Adapted and rearranged with poetic license after *Carmina Gadelica*.

A Charm to Divine by Firefly

Queen of the fireflies, hurry apace.
　　Come to me now as if running a race.

Bridle the horse as to you I now sing.
　　Bridle, O bridle the son of the king.

Under a glass, no secret concealed,
　　to me, your mysteries shall be revealed.

To every last mystery I shall attain,
　　even to that at the last of the grain.

Origin: 1800s or earlier. Italian. Adapted and rearranged with poetic license after *Aradia: Gospel of the Witches of Italy*.

A Charm to Open the Gates of the Sabbat

In the days when the Old Ones walked,
 Endymion lay cursed in his bed.

Tana called in the moonlight
 to charm a place out of their dreaming.

Three crosses on his bed she made
 to fix the gate to the sabbat-realm

so that the unwise could not enter
 and no power of sleep or death

could part them. So do I draw open
 the gates of the dreaming sabbat

to dwell for a time in that fair land.

Origin: 1800s or earlier. Italian. Adapted and rearranged with poetic license after *Aradia: Gospel of the Witches of Italy.*

A Seeker's Charm

As Old Etta Baines, Pellar of Art did call
    upon her powers of seeking and finding

to fix her eye upon the dwelling
    of any thief, as sure as the hawk

spies the rodent in the field at noon,
    by that same art do I call upon

the sight to serve me, so help me.

Origin: Most likely 1800s. American. Adapted and rearranged
with poetic license after *The Silver Bullet*.

A Charm for Skin-changing

And I shall go into a hare
  with sorrow and sighing and muckle care,

and I shall go in the Devil's name
  until I come home again.

And I shall go into a crow
  with sorrow and sighing and blackest throw,

and I shall go in the Devil's name
  until I come home again.

And I shall go into a cat
  with sorrow and sighing and a black shot,

and I shall go in the Devil's name
  until I come home again.

Origin: 17th century. Scottish. Adapted and rearranged with
poetic license after The Confessions of Isobel Gowdie.

A Latinate Charm for Visions or Dreams

Quis ascendet in montem domini?
    Aut quis stabit in loco sancto ejus?

Attollite portas, principes, vestras, et elevamini,
    portae aeternales, et introibit rex gloriae.

Quis est iste rex gloriae? Dominus fortis
    et potens, dominus potens in praelio.

Attollite portas, principes, vestras, et elevamini,
    portae aeternales, et introibit rex gloriae.

Quis est iste rex gloriae? Dominus virtutum
    ipse est rex gloriae.

Origin: 5th century B.C.E. Pagan, Canaan. Adapted and
rearranged with poetic license after the *Book of Psalms* (Vulgate)
and the *Sixth and Seventh Books of Moses*.

A Charm for Witch-flight

Come a stone horse, and come a stone mare.
  Gray mane, gray tail, gray stripe down her back.

From saddle to stirrup, I'll mount ye again,
  and on my ten toes, I'll ride over the plain.

Origin: 1800s or earlier. American or possibly British Isles.
Adapted and rearranged with poetic license after *Wehman Bros'*
Good Old-Time Songs, No. 1.

A Witch-fire Charm

And in the dark wood did Old Kate Hiller
    go forth as a ball of fire and light,

seeking out the enemy in the night,
    sowing what charms she may beneath

the branches of shadowed trees, roving
    as an orb of light, a will-o-wisp

of bright witch fire. And so do I call upon
    that very living flame to carry me now.

Origin: Most likely 1800s. American. Adapted and rearranged
with poetic license after *The Silver Bullet*.

A Sibylline Charm

Sambetta, give to me thy voice.
    Libussa, give to me thy voice.

Atemis, give to me thy voice.
    Cumana, give to me thy voice.

Eritrean, give to me thy voice.
    Fito, give to me thy voice.

Amaltea, give to me thy voice.
    Elespontiaca, give to me thy voice.

Frigia, give to me thy voice.
    Tiburtina, give to me thy voice.

Origin: 1700s. French. Adapted and rearranged with poetic license after *The Grimoirium Verum.*

A Cartomantic Charm

I call on the carding arts of Old Liz Gootchin,
    in whose name I enchant this pack

to seek out the answers my heart demands
    as surely as a pack of wild dogs

will snarl and snap in pursuit of prey.

Origin: Most likely 1800s. American. Adapted and rearranged
with poetic license after *The Silver Bullet.*

A Charm for Speaking with the Dead

Here do I call those powers infernal
     which sit enthroned in their dark abodes.

Come. Leave behind your dwellings
     behind the river Styx, and demonstrate

your powers now. Bring forth the one I seek
     named [Name] in this very place and hour.

Ad me venite, mortui. Ego sum qui te peto,
     et videre quero.

Origin: 1700s. French. Adapted and rearranged with poetic
license after *The Grimoirium Verum.*

A Chant for Witch-flight

Horse and hattock,
  horse and go.

Horse and pellatis,
  ho, ho.

[Repeat]

Origin: 17th century. Scottish. Adapted and rearranged with
poetic license after The Confessions of Isobel Gowdie.

A Chant to Open the Black Book of the Art

Obymero, per noctem
   et Symeam et membres membris

et Lasys cawtis
   nomis et Arypis.

[Repeat]

Origin: 16th century. English. Adapted and rearranged with
poetic license after Folgers Manuscript V.b.26.

A Chant for Journeying to the Sabbat

Thout a tout tout.
    Throughout and about.

Thout a tout tout.
    Throughout and about.

[Repeat]

Origin: 17th Century. British Isles. Adapted and rearranged with poetic license after *Saducismus Triumphatus*.

A Chant for the Ecstasy of the Sabbat

Bazabi lacha bachabe
    Lamac cahi achabahe
      Karrelyos

Lamac Lamec Bachalyos
    Cabahagy Sabalyos
      Baryolas

Lagoz atha Cabyolas
    Samacha atha Famolas
      Hurrahya
      Hurrahya
      Hurrahya

Origin: 13th Century. Basque. Adapted and rearranged with poetic license after *Le Miracle de Theophile*.

A Chant to Anoint a Divinatory Tool

Descendat spiritus
in hoc speculum.

Descendat spiritus
in hoc speculum.

[Repeat]

Origin: 16th century. English. Adapted and rearranged with
poetic license after Folgers Manuscript V.b.26.

A Chant to Bring Visions or Dreams

Agla leta
  yskyros mediator

eleyson panton
  craton.

Agla leta
  yskyros mediator

eleyson panton
  craton.

[Repeat]

Origin: 16th century. English. Adapted and rearranged with poetic license after Folgers Manuscript V.b.26.

Blessings and Benedictions

A Traveling Charm

Irly, walk thou beside me.
  Terly, walk thou beside me.

Erly, walk thou beside me.
  Baltazard, walk thou beside me.

Melchior, walk thou beside me.
  Gaspard, walk thou beside me.

Origin: 1700s. French. Adapted and rearranged with poetic license after *The Grimoirium Verum*.

A Charm with Yarrow

I will pick the smooth yarrow
    that my shape may charm,

that my lips may charm,
    that my voice may charm.

May I be like an island in the sea,
    or like a hill upon the land.

May I be like a star
    when the moon is waning.

I shall wound every man.
    No man shall wound me.

Origin: 1700s to 1800s or earlier. Scottish. Adapted and rearranged with poetic license after *Carmina Gadelica*.

A Charm for Healing and Blessing by Water (Lustration)

A palmful for thine health,
   a palmful for thy strength,

a palmful for thy growth,
   a palmful for thy beauty,

a palmful for thy bones,
   a palmful for thy feet,

a palmful for thy legs,
   a palmful for thine hands,

a palmful for thine arms,
   a palmful for thy chest,

a palmful for thy belly,
   a palmful for thy neck

a palmful for thy face,
    a palmful for thine head,

a palmful for thine arms,
    a palmful for thy blood,

a palmful for thy sinews,
    and a flood for thine appetite.

Origin: 1700s to 1800s or earlier. Scottish. Adapted and rearranged with poetic license after *Carmina Gadelica*.

Another Lustration Charm

A palmful for thine age,
    a palmful for thy growth,

a palmful for thy throat,
    a flood for thine appetite.

For thy share of the bounty,
    crowdie and kail;

For thy share of the taking,
    honey and warm milk.

For thy share of the supping,
    whisked whey and fat;

For thy share of the spoil,
    with bow and with spear.

For thy share of the preparation,
    the yellow eggs of Easter;

For thy share of the treat,
    my treasure and my joy.

For thy share of the feast
    with gifts and with tribute;

For thy share of the treasure,
    pulset of my love.

For thy share of the chase
    up the face of Beinn-a-cheo;

For thy share of the hunting
    and the ruling over hosts.

For thy share of palaces
    and the courts of kings;

For thy share of paradise
    with its goodness and its peace.

The part of thee that does not grow at dawn,
    may it grow at eventide;

The part of thee that does not grow at night,
    may it grow at ridge of middle-day.

Three palmfuls to preserve thee
    from every envy, evil eye, and death:

three palmfuls of the sacred waters
    of life, of love, and of peace.

Origin: 1700s to 1800s or earlier. Scottish. Adapted and
rearranged with poetic license after *Carmina Gadelica*.

A Guarding Charm

May Mary the mild keep thee.
  May Brigid the calm keep thee.

May Columba keep thee.
  May Maolruba keep thee.

May Carmac keep thee
  from the wolf in the night.

May Oran keep thee.
  May Modan keep thee.

May Dorman keep thee.
  May Moluag keep thee.

May Maolruan keep thee
  on soft land and hard land,

on earth, sea, and sky.
  May the spirit of peace preserve thee

from wounding, sickness, and death.

Origin: 1700s to 1800s or earlier. Scottish. Adapted and rearranged with poetic license after *Carmina Gadelica*.

A Black Paternoster

Black Paternoster,
    in darkness I prosper.

Balthazar, Melchior,
    and Casper.

Guide me by night,
    and be my protector

as long as I keep
    thy Black Paternoster.

Original. Grounded in Early Modern Scottish folklore.

A Blue Paternoster

Blue Paternoster,
    Janet's sweet foster,

mother of cunning
    and first clew-caster,

grant the desire
    my heart seeks after

for well do I know
    thy Blue Paternoster.

Original. Grounded in Early Modern Scottish folklore.

A White Paternoster

White Paternoster,
  stronger and faster

than harm by foe
  and all disaster.

Come trumpet and soldier,
  Come mistress and master,

as I now speak
  the White Paternoster.

Original. Grounded in Early Modern Scottish folklore.

A Green Paternoster

Green Paternoster,
　Mary's dear sister

who knew every charm
　of midwife and healer,

be thou my guardian,
　be thou my foster

as long as I know
　thy Green Paternoster.

Original. Grounded in Early Modern Scottish folklore.

A Kindling of the Light of Protection

Here I set a fire bright
    with Brigid and Mary in its light,

upon the ceiling and the floor,
    on every wall and every door.

Origin: 1700s to 1800s or earlier. Scottish. Adapted and
rearranged with poetic license after *Carmina Gadelica*.

A Chant to Consecrate a Magic Circle

Coniuro te circulum
    et consecro locum istum.

Coniuro te circulum
    et consecro locum istum.

[Repeat]

Origin: 16th century. English. Adapted and rearranged with poetic license after Folgers Manuscript V.b.26.

Charm of the Caim
or Ring of Protection

Before me, Sain.
    Behind me, Sain.

Above me, Sain.
    Below me, Sain.

To my right, Sain.
    To my left, Sain.

Origin: 1700s to 1800s or earlier. Scottish. Adapted and rearranged with poetic license after *Carmina Gadelica*.

A Charm for Safe Travels

Wisdom be in my thoughts
    and in my speech,

and vitality linger on my lips
    until I journey home again.

Traversing corries,
    traversing forests,

traversing valleys long and wild,
    Moon uphold me.

Sun uphold me.
    Stars uphold me.

Earth uphold me.
    Sea uphold me.

Sky uphold me.
   Brigid and Mary uphold me.

Origin: 1700s to 1800s or earlier. Scottish. Adapted and
rearranged with poetic license after *Carmina Gadelica*.

A Charm against Sickness

Sickness, vanish into the heavens.
  Suffering, rise up to the clouds.

Vapor, fly upon the air,
  dispersed by wind and storm.

Neither the sun nor the moon
  shall give thee light.

The wind shall hold thee
  from inflicting injury to flesh.

Origin: Unknown antiquity. Finnish. Adapted and rearranged
with poetic license after *Kalevala*.

A Charm against Bleeding

Hear me, blood, and obey.
    Withhold thy warm stream

and halt thy red flow.
    Blood, be stopped as by a wall.

Blood, be stopped as by a hedge.
    Blood, be stopped as by a reef

in the deep, dark sea,
    a sedge stiff in the moss,

a stone fixed in a hillside,
    a pine tree rooted in the earth.

Origin: Unknown antiquity. Finnish. Adapted and rearranged
with poetic license after *Kalevala*.

A Charm to Cut through Illusions

Once, an Old One split the mist,
   his sword dripping mead and honey.

The fog departed from the lake-waves
   as he clove the thickness of air.

So, too, do I divide by art
   the vapor that conceals my sight.

Origin: Unknown antiquity. Finnish. Adapted and rearranged with poetic license after *Kalevala*.

A Blessing Upon an Article of Clothing

Well do I know my rahn, my rahn
    in wood and glen and by the sea.

Rahn of one:
    the charm is come.

Rahn of two:
    I conjure you.

Rahn of three:
    My will to be.

Rahn of four:
    Ceiling to floor.

Rahn of five:
    It comes alive.

Rahn of six:
    My will to fix.

My rahn of seven,
    A charm be given

as milk unto the calf.
    By my rahn of seven-and-a-half,

who wears this cloth shall not be wounded.
    It shall not be torn in any battle.

This is a charm known by no priest.
    It is the charm given in secret

of the cresses, the stones, the deer, the salmon,
    and by these I conjure it,

this sanctuary shield.

Origin: 1700s to 1800s or earlier. Scottish. Adapted and
rearranged with poetic license after *Carmina Gadelica*.

A Charm of the White Serpent

White serpent of old, I conjure you
    of palest scales, wise worm of art

who did carry three leaves to the ruined
    body of thy mate, mending

torn flesh with your craft as surely
    as white-hot metal is beat together,

shards of iron becoming one again,
    you whose flesh blesses the tongue

to speak the languages of all creatures,
    lightning of wisdom, sea-crest of cunning.

Original. Grounded in European folklore. See *The White Serpent*
and *The Serpent's Leaves* by the Brothers Grimm.

A Charm of Lasting Life

Upon this body, I place the charm
    for prosperity, life, and protection.

It is the charm that Brigid lay
    around the fair neck of Dornghil

between sole and throat,
    between pap and knee,

between back and breast,
    between chest and sole,

between eye and hair.
    Nothing between heaven, earth, and hell

can overcome it.
    No spear shall overcome it.

No sea shall overcome it.
    No human act shall overcome it.

This body shall ascend the hill
    as the calm swan amidst violence.

Stand thou against five hundred,
    and thine oppressors shall be seized.

Origin: 1700s to 1800s or earlier. Scottish. Adapted and
rearranged with poetic license after *Carmina Gadelica*.

A Charm for Protection against the Evil Eye

Here do I trample upon the eye of my enemy
    who would seek to do me harm.

As tramples the duck upon the lake,
    the swan upon the water,

the horse upon the plain,
    the cow upon the field,

the host of the elements,
    so do I crush and scatter

a portion of it upon the gray stones,
    a portion upon the steep hills,

a portion upon the fast falls,
    a portion upon the fair meads,

and a portion upon the salty sea,
    and she, at last, shall drown it fast.

Origin: 1700s to 1800s or earlier. Scottish. Adapted and rearranged with poetic license after *Carmina Gadelica*.

A Blessing for Beer and Whiskey

Three men came out of the West,
  their fortunes for to try,

and these three swore a solemn vow:
  John Barleycorn must die.

They ploughed and sowed and harrowed him,
  poured clods upon his head

til these three men were satisfied
  John Barleycorn was dead.

They let him stand til Midsummer day
  when he looked both pale and wan;

John Barleycorn grew a long, long beard,
  and so became a man.

They hired men with their scythes so sharp
  to cut him off at the knee;

They rolled him and tied him around the waist,
    and served him barbarously.

They hired men with their sharp pitchforks
    to pierce him in the heart,

but the loader did serve him worse than that,
    for he bound him to the cart.

They hired men with their crab-tree sticks
    to split him skin from bone,

but the miller did serve him worse than that,
    for he ground him between stones.

The huntsman cannot hunt the fox,
    nor loudly blow his horn,

and the tinker cannot mend his pots
    without John Barleycorn.

Origin: 17th Century. British Isles. Adapted and rearranged with poetic license after *A Pleasant New Ballad to Sing Both Euen and Morne*.

A Charm with Wine

It is not wine I drink in this glass,
    but the blood of the queen of witches all

to pulse through the vines of my body.
    I kiss my hand to the moon

and pray that she will watch over
    my house, my harvest, and my craft

and bring good fortune to my land.

Origin: 1800s or earlier. Italian. Adapted and rearranged with
poetic license after *Aradia: Gospel of the Witches of Italy*.

A Latinate Charm for Luck

Cum invocarem exaudivit me deus iustitiae meae:
  in tribulatione dilatasti mihi.

Miserere mei, et exaudi orationem meam.
  Et scitote quoniam mirificavit dominus sanctum

suum: dominus exaudiet me cum clamavero ad eum.
  Signatum est super nos lumen vultus tui domine:

dedisti laetitiam in corde meo.
  A fructu frumenti, vini,

et olei sui multiplicati sunt.
  In pace in idipsum dormiam, et requiescam.

Origin: 5th century B.C.E. Pagan, Canaan. Adapted and
rearranged with poetic license after the *Book of Psalms* (Vulgate)
and the *Sixth and Seventh Books of Moses*.

A Latinate Charm of Protection

In te domine speravi non confundar
    in aeternum: in iustitia tua libera me.

Inclina ad me aurem tuam, accelera ut eruas me.
    Esto mihi in deum protectorem:

et in domum refugii, ut salvum me facias.
    Educes me de laqueo hoc, quem absconderunt

mihi: quoniam tu es protector meus.
    Odisti observantes vanitates, supervacue.

Ego autem in domino speravi.
    Oblivioni datus sum tamquam mortuus a corde.

Factus sum tamquam vas perditum.
    In manibus tuis sortes meae.

Eripe me de manu inimicorum meorum,
    et a persequentibus me.

Origin: 5th century B.C.E. Pagan, Canaan. Adapted and
rearranged with poetic license after the *Book of Psalms* (Vulgate)
and the *Sixth and Seventh Books of Moses*.

A Latinate Charm of Freedom from All Bindings

Suscipiant montes pacem populo: et colles iustitiam.
    Iudicabit pauperes populi, et salvos faciet filios

pauperum: et humiliabit calumniatorem.
    Et permanebit cum sole, et ante lunam,

in generatione et generationem.
    Descendet sicut pluvia in vellus: et sicut

stillicidia stillantia super terram.
    Orietur in diebus eius iustitia, et abundantia pacis:

donec auferatur luna.
    Et dominabitur a mari usque ad mare: et a flumine

usque ad terminos orbis terrarum.
    Quia liberabit pauperem a potente:

et pauperem cui non erat adiutor.

.

Origin: 5th century B.C.E. Pagan, Canaan. Adapted and rearranged with poetic license after the *Book of Psalms* (Vulgate) and the *Sixth and Seventh Books of Moses*.

A Latinate Charm against Dire Illness

Priusquam montes fierent, aut formaretur terra,
  et orbis: a saeculo et usque in saeculum tu es deus.

Mane sicut herba transeat, mane floreat, et transeat:
  vespere decidat, induret, et arescat.

Quia defecimus in ira tua, et in furore
  tuo turbati sumus.

Quoniam omnes dies nostri defecerunt:
  et in ira tua defecimus.

Anni nostri sicut aranea meditabuntur.
  Convertere domine usquequo?

Et deprecabilis esto super servos tuos.
  Laetati sumus pro diebus,

quibus nos humiliasti:
>   annis, quibus vidimus mala.

Origin: 5th century B.C.E. Pagan, Canaan. Adapted and rearranged with poetic license after the *Book of Psalms* (Vulgate) and the *Sixth and Seventh Books of Moses*.

A Chant to Anoint a Simulacrum

Ailif casyl azaze
    hit mel meltat.

Ailif casyl azaze
    hit mel meltat.

[Repeat]

Origin: Early Modern. British Isles. Adapted and rearranged
with poetic license after *The Discoverie of Witchcraft*.

A Chant to Cleanse Unwanted Influences

Asperges me hyssopo domine et mundabor
  Lavabis me, et supernivem dealbabor

Asperges me hyssopo domine et mundabor
  Lavabis me, et supernivem dealbabor

[Repeat]

Origin: 5th century B.C.E. Pagan, Canaan. Adapted and
rearranged with poetic license after the *Book of Psalms* (Vulgate)